DATE DUE

1998	

PRINTED IN U.S.A.

The United States

Minnesota

Paul Joseph
ABDO & Daughters

visit us at
www.abdopub.com

Published by Abdo & Daughters, 4940 Viking Drive, Suite 622, Edina, Minnesota 55435.
Copyright © 1998 by Abdo Consulting Group, Inc., Pentagon Tower, P.O. Box 36036, Minneapolis, Minnesota 55435 USA. International copyrights reserved in all countries. No part of this book may be reproduced in any form without written permission from the publisher.

Printed in the United States.

Cover and Interior Photo credits: Peter Arnold, Inc., Corbis-Bettman, Archive Photos, Super Stock

Edited by Lori Kinstad Pupeza
Contributing editor Brooke Henderson
Special thanks to our Checkerboard Kids—Brandon Isakson, Aisha Baker, John Hansen, Stephanie McKenna

All statistics taken from the 1990 census; The Rand McNally Discovery Atlas of The United States. Other sources: Compton's Encyclopedia, 1997; *Minnesota*, Heinrichs, Children's Press, Chicago, 1989.

Library of Congress Cataloging-in-Publication Data

Joseph, Paul, 1970-
       Minnesota / Paul Joseph.
       p. cm. -- (United States)
       Includes index.
       Summary: Surveys the history, geography, and people of and interesting facts about the state known as "The Land of 10,000 Lakes."
       ISBN 1-56239-863-6
       1. Minnesota--Juvenile literature. [1. Minnesota.] I. Title. II. Series: United States (Series)
       F606.3.J66   1998
       977.6--dc21

                                         97-11734
                                       CIP
                                       AC

Contents

Welcome to Minnesota

Minnesota is filled with thousands and thousands of lakes. The state is known as the "Land of 10,000 Lakes." Besides lakes, Minnesota offers beautiful natural landscapes. There are valleys, prairies, wilderness areas, high bluffs, and rocky shores.

Minnesota was named after the Minnesota River. The Dakota **Native Americans** called the river Minisota. The word means cloudy or milky water.

Minnesota is a rich farming community. At one time **mining** was the biggest industry in the state. Today, **manufacturing** is the biggest. Farming, however, has always been one of the biggest businesses and continues to be.

The small rural communities are a staple in the state. But Minnesota also has big cities like the Twin Cities, Minneapolis and St. Paul. Each city, separated by the

Mississippi River, has wonderful museums, excellent theaters, beautiful parks and lakes, and a lively downtown.

The state of Minnesota is a growing state with many things to do. It also has a rich history that is very interesting.

Minnesota is the "Land of 10,000 Lakes."

Fast Facts

MINNESOTA

Capital
St. Paul (272,235 people)
Area
79,548 square miles
(206,028 sq km)
Population
4,387,029 people
Rank: 20th
Statehood
May 11, 1858
(32nd state admitted)
Principal rivers
Mississippi River
Red River
Minnesota River
Highest point
Eagle Mountain; 2,301 feet
(701 m)
Largest city
Minneapolis (368,383 people)
Motto
L'Etoile du nord
(The north star)
Song
"Hail! Minnesota"
Famous People
F. Scott Fitzgerald, Hubert
Humphrey, Sinclair Lewis,
Walter Mondale, Charles Schulz

*S*tate Flag

*P*ink-and-white
Lady's Slipper

*C*ommon Loon

*R*ed Pine

About Minnesota

The North Star State

Detail area

CANADA

N. Dakota

Minnesota

Lake Superior

S. Dakota

Wisconsin

Iowa

MN
Minnesota's abbreviation

Borders: west (N. Dakota, S. Dakota), north (Canada), east (Wisconsin, Lake Superior), south (Iowa)

Nature's Treasures

Minnesota is known for its thousands of lakes. It also has wonderful forests, beautiful parks, rich farmland, and many natural treasures.

Minnesota has two national forests and more acres of state forests than any other state. About half of the state's total land area is farms. There are only four other states that have more farms in it.

Minnesota is also known for its **mineral**-rich ground. Minnesota is a leader in the **production** of **iron ore**.

The state of Minnesota has lakes filled with fish, rivers, bluffs, wilderness areas, and hills for skiing. Minnesota's sky-blue waters that are scattered throughout the state, along with its pleasant summer months, are Minnesota's finest treasure.

An iron mine in northern Minnesota.

Beginnings

Cave men lived in Minnesota many thousands of years ago. At one time the state was covered in huge glaciers of ice. This was known as the Ice Age. After it melted, Minnesota was mostly covered with deep forests and lakes.

The first **explorers** in the state found **Native Americans** living in the region. The Dakota, also known as the Lakota or the Sioux, were found living in forests. Later explorers discovered the Chippewa, or Ojibwa as they were also called.

Two Frenchmen, who came to hunt furs around the 1650s, were the first explorers to reach Minnesota. They were Pierre Esprit Radisson, and Médard Chouart. Most of Minnesota was claimed by France.

After the French and Indian War, France gave the land east of the Mississippi to England. In 1783, England gave most of Minnesota to the United States. Twenty years later the United States owned all of Minnesota.

Many **settlers** began moving into Minnesota in the 1850s. People from New York, Pennsylvania, and New England were moving west for land.

On May 11, 1858, Minnesota became the 32nd state. At the time, 150,000 people lived there. In less than 10 years it grew to almost 500,000 people

Pierre Esprit Radisson was a French fur trader and explorer.

B.C. to 1700

Many thousands of years ago, during the Ice Age, Minnesota was covered with glaciers. After the Ice Age, Minnesota was filled with forests and lakes.

The first people known to live on the land were **Native Americans**. They were the Dakota, also known as the Lakota or the Sioux, and the Chippewa, or Ojibwa.

1654-1660: Pierre Esprit Radisson and Médard Chouart are the first European **explorers** to visit Minnesota.

1679: Daniel Greysolon claims the area for France.

Minnesota
B.C. to 1700

13

1700s to 1800s

 1803: All of Minnesota is owned by the United States.

 1847: The first settlement is made on what is now Minneapolis.

 1851: The University of Minnesota is opened in Minneapolis.

 1858: Minnesota becomes the 32nd state, on May 11. St. Paul is named the capital.

 1889: The Mayo Clinic is established in Rochester.

Minnesota
1700s to 1800s

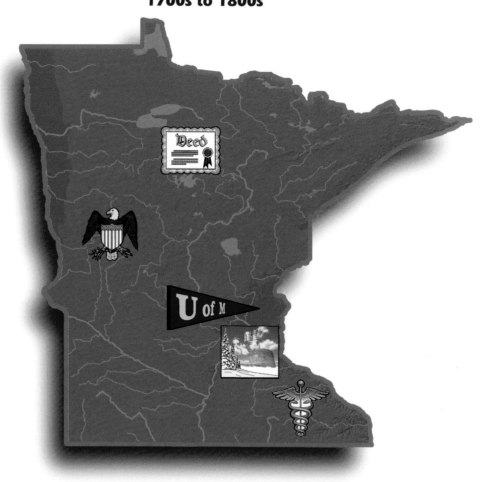

The 1900s

 1964: **Senator** Hubert H. Humphrey of Minnesota is elected vice president of the United States.

 1965: Horrible floods destroys communities along the Mississippi River.

 1976: Senator Walter Mondale of Minnesota is elected vice president of the United States.

 1991: The Minnesota Twins win a second World Series in less than four years.

 1992: Minneapolis hosts the Super Bowl.

Minnesota
The 1900s

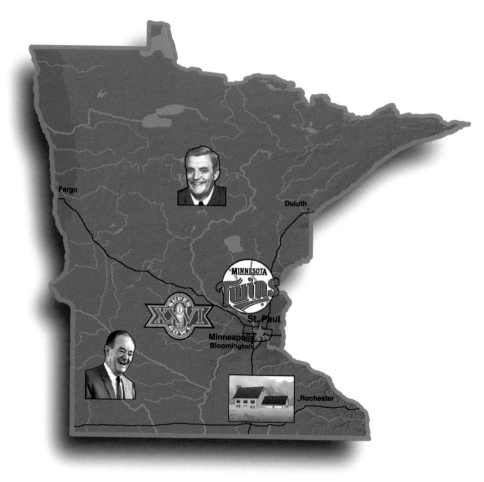

Fargo

Duluth

MINNESOTA
Twins

SUPER
XXVI
BOWL

St. Paul

Minneapolis
Bloomington

.Rochester

Minnesota's People

There are about 4.4 million people in Minnesota. It is the 20th biggest state. Most of the people in the state are white. Less than two percent are African American. About one percent of the state is **Native American**.

Many well-known people have made Minnesota home. The most famous is Hubert H. Humphrey. He was the Minneapolis **mayor**, then he became a **senator**. Later he became the vice president of the United States.

Another **politician**, Walter Mondale, was also a senator from Minnesota. Mondale was also the vice president of the United States. In 1980, he ran for president and lost.

Warren Burger was chief justice of the Supreme Court from 1969-1986. He was also from Minnesota.

The founder of the Sears stores was born in Stewartville, Minnesota. Richard Sears started a mail-order business in 1886. Today, Sears department stores are all over the United States.

Many entertainers are from Minnesota. The creator of "Peanuts," Charles Schulz, is from Minneapolis, Minnesota. Judy Garland, who played Dorothy in *The Wizard of Oz* and was in many other movies, was born in Grand Rapids, Minnesota. Bob Dylan, a musician from the 1960s lived in Hibbing. And the singer that used to be called Prince was born in Minneapolis and now lives in Chanhassen.

Charles Schulz

Judy Garland (c)

Hubert H. Humphrey

Splendid Cities

Minnesota doesn't have a lot of large cities. There are many small farming towns and many medium sized cities. The state is famous, however, for its Twin Cities.

The Twin Cities of Minneapolis and St. Paul are separated by the Mississippi River. The Twin Cities are famous for being alike and also for being near the top of the Mississippi River. But the two cities are very unique in their own way.

Minneapolis is Minnesota's largest city. In the middle of this city is a wonderful chain of lakes where people jog, walk, and rollerblade. People also swim, sail, and fish in these lakes. Minneapolis is also home to the Minnesota Twins, Vikings, and Timberwolves.

Duluth

St. Paul

Minneapolis

Rochester

20

The city of St. Paul is the capital of Minnesota. The city is crowned by the beautiful state capitol building. St. Paul has many excellent small colleges such as Hamline, St. Thomas, and Macalester.

Bloomington is the third largest, and Duluth is the fourth largest city. It is on Lake Superior in northeastern Minnesota. It has a fine university and a nice downtown.

Rochester may very well be the most notable city in Minnesota. It is the home to the Mayo Clinic. Many people come to this world-famous clinic including presidents, entertainers, athletes, Kings, Queens, and everyday people for health reasons.

Beautiful Minneapolis sits along the Mississippi River.

Minnesota's Land

    Minnesota's land is mostly lakes, prairies, swamps, and hills. The state is divided into two distinct regions: the Central Lowlands and the Superior Upland.

    The Central Lowland covers all but the northeast part of the state. This area has a variety of features. There are flat plains in the Red River valley. There is a forest and lake section.

    The Central Lowland also features the Big Woods. The Big Woods has thousands of lakes and many evergreen forests.

    The Minnesota River crosses the southern area of the Central Lowland. The southern area also features rolling prairies, wooded hills, deep valleys, and excellent farmland.

    The Superior Upland is the area in northeast Minnesota. It is a forested area of lakes and ridges. Rainy

Lake is on its northern border. And Lake Superior is on the east. Towards the west are thousands of small lakes.

The biggest rivers in this region are the St. Louis and the St. Croix. Here also is the highest and lowest points in the state. Eagle Mountain, at 2,301 feet (701 m), is the highest. The lowest is 602 feet (183 m) at Lake Superior.

Minnesota has beautiful lakes and forests.

Minnesota at Play

The people of Minnesota and the visitors to this wonderful state enjoy many things to do. The sky-blue lakes, dense forests, and pleasant summers have made it a great place to play.

The state is great for hunting, hiking, and of course fishing. Most people in Minnesota live near a lake. This makes for many water activities. Swimming, skiing, and sailboarding are just a few fun things to do on a lake.

Away from the lake people love to golf. There are more golf courses in the state of Minnesota than any other state in the country.

In the winter months people continue to use the lakes. People snowmobile, ice fish, and ice skate. People also ski at the many ski resorts in Minnesota.

Besides outdoor activities, Minnesota offers many things to do inside. Tourists have made the Mall of America in Bloomington the most visited shopping area in the world. It has thousands of stores and restaurants, four huge department stores, 14 movie screens, and an amusement park with a roller coaster and log ride. All of this is under one roof!

The largest shopping mall in America is in Minnesota.

Minnesota at Work

The people of Minnesota must work to make money. For a long time many people in the state worked on the **iron range**. At one time, Minnesota provided most of America's **iron ore**. In the 1950s, however, most of the supply was dwindled to low amounts.

Today, Minnesota is still among the major **mineral producing** states. It produces high-grade ore, sand, gravel, and granite.

Farming is a huge business in Minnesota. Farming is one of the leading jobs in the state. About half of the state's total land area has farms on it. A lot of corn is grown in Minnesota. Farmers also grow wheat, barley, and soybeans. Farms that raise cows produce milk and beef.

The **manufacturing** business is the state's biggest business. Manufacturing has outdone farming since the 1950s. Meat-packing plants **process** cows. Mills grind wheat and other grains into flour. Minneapolis is a leader in flour **production**.

Many people work in the large businesses of 3M, Honeywell, General Mills, Pillsbury, and Land O'Lakes, which are all in Minnesota.

Because of its beauty, people, land, and lakes, Minnesota is a great place to visit, live, work, and play.

Corn harvesting in Minnesota.

Fun Facts

•The highest point in Minnesota is Eagle Mountain. It is 2,301 feet (701 meters) tall. The lowest point is Lake Superior. It is only 602 feet (183 meters).

•Minnesota is the 14th largest state. Its land covers 79,548 square miles (206,028 sq km). In population, however, it is only the 20th biggest state.

•The city of St. Paul was named after the first church built in the city. However, the city had a different name before that—it was called Pig's Eye!

•More people ice fish in the state of Minnesota than any other state. People even drive cars and put up little houses on the lakes when the ice gets thick enough.

Ice fishermen in northern Minnesota.

Glossary

Explorers: people that are one of the first to discover and look over land.

Iron Ore: a type of mineral found in parts of Minnesota.

Iron Range: the northeastern area of Minnesota.

Manufacture: to make things by machine in a factory.

Mayor: the highest elected official of a city.

Minerals: things found in the earth, such as rock, diamonds, or coal.

Mining: working underground to get minerals.

Native Americans: the first people who were born in and occupied North America.

Politician: an elected official who makes laws for the city, county, state, or country.

Process: to make into something.

Produce: to make something.

Products: things made that will be sold to people.

Settlers: people that move to a new land where no one has lived before and build a community.

Senator: one of two elected officials from a state that represents the state in Washington D.C. There they make laws and are part of Congress.

Senate: also known as congress, is a group of 100 elected senators (two from each state) that represent their state and make laws for the country.

Internet Sites

Minnesota Online

http://www.mnonline.org

MN Online, a guide to Minnesota's Internet, is an award-winning online information service. Each week, MN Online's editors highlight and review the most useful, creative, and noteworthy sites in Minnesota.

These sites are subject to change. Go to your favorite search engine and type in Minnesota for more sites.

PASS IT ON

Tell Others Something Special About Your State

To educate readers around the country, pass on interesting tips, places to see, history, and little unknown facts about the state you live in. We want to hear from you!

To get posted on ABDO & Daughters website
E-mail us at "mystate@abdopub.com"

Index